W

HONEYBEE

Life Cycles

Jason Cooper

Rourke

www.rourkepublishing.com

PHOTO CREDITS:
Cover, pp. 4, 7, 8, 18, 19, 20, 22 (stage 4) © Lynn M. Stone; p. 6 © James H. Carmichael; p. 16 © Breck P. Kent; pp. 10, 12, 13, 14, 22 (stages1, 2, and 3) © Kim Taylor/Bruce Coleman, Inc.

Editor: Frank Sloan

Cover and page design by Nicola Stratford

Library of Congress Cataloging-in-Publication Data

Cooper, Jason, 1942-
  Honeybee / Jason Cooper.
       p. cm. -- (Life cycles)
Summary: Describes the physical characteristics, habitat, behavior, life cycle, diet, and reproduction of these industrious producers of honey. Includes bibliographical references (p.   ).
  ISBN 1-58952-705-4 (hardcover)
  1. Honeybee--Juvenile literature. [1. Honeybee. 2. Bees.] 1. Title.
II. Series: Cooper, Jason, 1942-   Life cycles.
  QL568.A6C58 2003
  595.79'9--dc21
                                    2003011550

Printed in the USA

CG/CG

Table of Contents

Honeybees make so much honey that beekeepers can take some without starving the bees.

Honeybees

Everyone knows the honeybee. It is one of our most familiar insects. Honeybees buzzing around flower blossoms are common sights and sounds.

Everyone knows about the honey that honeybees make, too. It is sweet and sticky. Honeybees make honey as food for themselves. But they make more than enough. **Beekeepers** take some of the bees' honey for people to eat.

Honeybees make honey from **nectar**. Nectar is a sweet liquid made by flowers. Honeybees suck nectar from the flowers. A honeybee has a long "tongue" that works like a straw. The bees store nectar in their stomachs. There it is changed into sugars.

Back at their home, called a **hive**, worker bees spit up the watery nectar. The water slowly becomes part of the air. What remains is honey!

A honeybee uses a strawlike tongue to sip nectar from flowers.

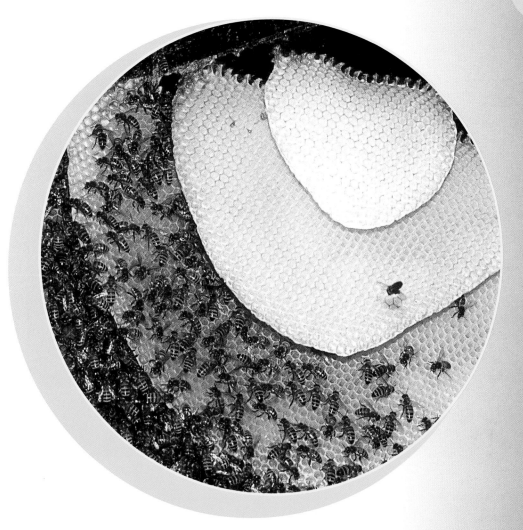

Wild honeybees swarm over the honeycomb sections of their hive.

The bees store the honey in the **honeycomb** they have made in the hive. The honeycomb is full of little storage **cells**.

Honeybees reach adulthood (shown here) only after going through life stages known as a metamorphosis.

From Egg to Adult

At birth, many of the animals you know best look very much like their parents. They are just smaller. Slowly, they gain length and weight and become adults.

Insects, however, don't look like their parents until they are grown up. And to grow up, they go through a series of life stages. At each stage, an insect looks different than its parents. All these stages of growing up are called insect **metamorphosis**.

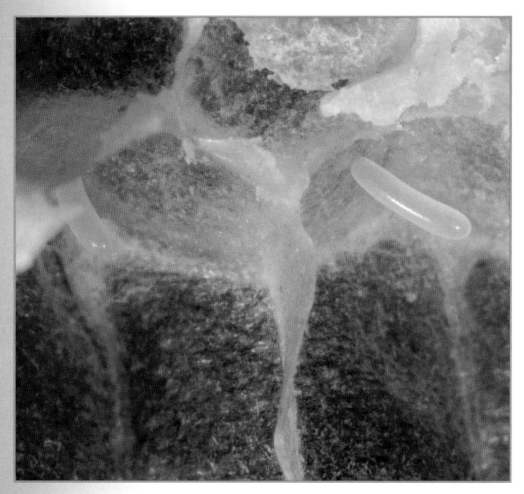

Honeybee eggs are the first step in metamorphosis.

The metamorphosis of the honeybee begins with a tiny, soft egg. The egg is the first stage of life.

Each honeybee egg is laid in a honeycomb cell. After three days, a worm-like **larva** crawls out of the egg. The larva is the honeybee's second life stage.

Worker bees feed the larva a mixture of honey and **pollen**. Pollen looks like yellow or orange dust.

Honeycomb cells here contain honeybee larvas and pupas.

Worker bees feed a honeybee queen.

Pollen is made by plants to help them **reproduce**. Honeybees collect pollen in special "baskets" on their legs.

The honeybee pupa is the last step in metamorphosis before becoming an adult.

The honeybee larva grows in its cell by eating for five days. Worker bees then cover the cell with beeswax. Inside the cell, the larva changes into another form, called the **pupa**.

The pupa stage lasts about two weeks. During that time, the pupa changes into an adult. The adult bee chews its way out of the cell.

Workers surround a queen bee, whose job is to lay eggs.

The Lives of Honeybees

Honeybees live and work together in groups of thousands. Each hive, however, has one special bee. She is the queen. She is bigger than other bees. Her job is to lay eggs. She does not defend the hive or search for nectar.

Most of the queen's offspring grow up to be either worker bees or drones. Workers are female bees, too. But they don't lay eggs. Instead, they fly off to find nectar and pollen. They make beeswax for the honeycomb. They feed the queen and the larva. Workers live from six weeks to several months.

Worker bees perform "dances" at the hive. Their dances help other workers know where to find certain flowers.

The greatest number of honeybees in any hive are workers, shown here with larvas.

A worker bee seeks nectar and pollen from a lily.

Drones are male bees. Their job is to mate with queen bees. Drones don't have stingers, and they can't feed themselves. Workers feed them until fall. By then food is scarce.

A drone (center) is bigger than workers, but it cannot feed itself.

Workers stop feeding the drones and pull them from the hive. The drones quickly die.

The queen bee may live for five years. During her lifetime, she may lay nearly one million eggs. Her many eggs help honeybees continue to be familiar sights and sounds.

Stage 1:
A honeybee begins
life in a tiny egg

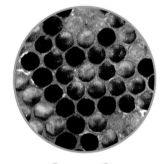

Stage 2:
A honeybee hatches
as a worm-like larva

Stage 3:
The larva becomes
a pupa

Stage 4:
The pupa becomes
an adult honeybee

Glossary

beekeepers (BEE KEEP urz) — people who keep and raise honeybees for their honey

cells (SELZ) — the compartments in a honeycomb

hive (HYV) — a place where bees stay, make honeycomb, and raise new bees

honeycomb (HUN ee KOM) — a waxy material made by bees and filled with little holes

larva (LAR vuh) — an early stage of growing up in insects when they look nothing like their parents

metamorphosis (MET uh MOR fuh sess) — a series of growth stages in which certain animals, such as insects, change into adults

nectar (NEK tur) — sweet liquid made by a flower

pollen (POLL un) — dust-like grains made by flowers to help make new flowers

pupa (PYU puh) — the stage of development between the larva and adult stages of many insects, including honeybees

reproduce (ree pro DYUS) — to make more of one's own kind

Index

Further Reading

Brimner, Larry Dane. *Bees*. Children's Press, 1999
Rustad, Martha E.H. *Honey Bees*. Pebble Books, 2003

Website to Visit

http://www.foodreference.com/html/fhoney.html

About the Author

Jason Cooper has written several children's books about a variety of topics for Rourke Publishing, including the recent series *Life Cycles* and *Fighting Forces*. Cooper travels widely to gather information for his books.